SUCCESSFUL AMERICANS

Vietnamese Americans

John F. Grabowski

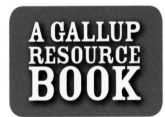

A GALLUP RESOURCE BOOK

Mason Crest Publishers
Philadelphia

Produced by OTTN Publishing in association with
Bow Publications, Inc.

MASON CREST PUBLISHERS INC.
370 Reed Road
Broomall, Pennsylvania 19008
(866) MCP-BOOK (toll free)
www.masoncrest.com

Printed in the United States of America.

First Printing

9 8 7 6 5 4 3 2 1

Library of Congress Cataloging-in-Publication Data

Grabowski, John F.
  Vietnamese Americans / John F. Grabowski.
     p. cm. — (Successful Americans)
  Includes bibliographical references.
  ISBN 978-1-4222-0522-8 (hardcover)
  ISBN 978-1-4222-0869-4 (pbk.)
  1. Vietnamese Americans—Biography—Juvenile literature. 2. Successful people—
United States—Biography—Juvenile literature. I. Title.
  F184.V53G73 2008
  973.92092'395922—dc22
                                                                  2008043956

Publisher's note:
All quotations in this book come from original sources, and contain the spelling
and grammatical inconsistencies of the original text.

◀ **CROSS-CURRENTS** ▶

When you see this logo, turn
to the Cross-Currents section
at the back of the book. The
Cross-Currents features explore
connections between people,
places, events, and ideas.

Table of Contents

The end of the Vietnam War, in 1975, led to mass emigration from Vietnam. Among the refugees were "boat people," who fled by sea in small vessels.

CHAPTER ONE

Vietnamese Immigration

In 2000, according to the U.S. Census Bureau, more than 1.2 million people of Vietnamese heritage lived in the United States. More than 988,000 of them were born in Vietnam. This makes them the fifth-largest immigrant group in the United States, after Mexican, Filipino, Chinese, and Asian Indian groups. Most Vietnamese immigrants came to the United States as a result of the Vietnam War, which began in 1959 and lasted until 1975.

WAR REFUGEES

Before 1975 very few Vietnamese immigrated to America. According to U.S. Immigration and Naturalization sources, the number who entered the country between 1950 and 1975 was significantly less than one thousand. Most were the wives and children of U.S. servicemen who saw action in Vietnam after the United States increased military aid to South Vietnam during the mid-1960s.

In 1965, fearing the establishment of a communist government in a unified Vietnam, the United States became involved in the Vietnam War. The U.S. government supported the military government of South Vietnam against the communist government of North Vietnam. During the course of the war, millions of Vietnamese civilians and members of the military lost their lives.

With the war's end, a new communist government came into power. The Vietnamese people who had sided with the Americans and the losing

South Vietnamese government, including government officials and military personnel, feared reprisals by the communists. Many of them fled to the United States. In April 1975, after the fall of Saigon, the capital of South Vietnam, the number of Vietnamese immigrating to the United States increased dramatically.

To help Vietnamese refugees enter the country and find places to live, the U.S. Congress passed and President Gerald Ford signed the Indochina Migration and Refugee Act in May 1975. Under this act approximately 120,000 Vietnamese entered the United States that year. They arrived at relocation centers in Fort Chaffee, Arkansas; Camp Pendleton, California; Eglin Air Force Base, Florida; and Fort Indiantown Gap, Pennsylvania. Many newcomers later made their way to the warmer

With the fall of the city of Saigon in April 1975, the U.S. government evacuated Americans and Vietnamese civilians by military transport plane.

climates of California and Texas, where they established their own communities.

Eventually the U.S. government granted the Vietnamese the legal right to stay in the United States. Senator Edward Kennedy sponsored a bill that changed the status of refugees from that of parolee (granted only temporary stay in the country) to that of permanent resident. The bill, known as the 1977 Adjustment of Status Clause, was added to the 1975 Indochina Migration and Refugee Act.

OPERATION BABYLIFT

Included among those evacuated from the country were orphaned and abandoned children. Many of them were born to American fathers and Vietnamese mothers. These Amerasian children were typically rejected by Vietnamese society. However, some organizations tried to help them by bringing them to the United States.

On April 3, 1975, President Gerald Ford announced the start of Operation Babylift. This effort would attempt to fly many of the estimated 70,000 orphans out of the war-ravished country. The humanitarian operation was not without its share of controversy. One U.S. social worker later recalled:

> Charges were made that removing children from their homeland and depriving them of their birth culture was American Cultural Imperialism. Some people insisted that the Vietnamese could have cared for the children had they been left in Vietnam. There were people opposed to transracial adoption.

President Gerald Ford signed off on Operation Babylift, a humanitarian mission headed by the U.S. government to evacuate Vietnamese orphans in 1975.

Vietnamese Immigration

Despite the objections more than 3,000 orphans were eventually transported to the United States and adopted by American families.

THE BOAT PEOPLE

For the people remaining in Vietnam under the new government, life was harsh. The country faced severe shortages of food and other basic necessities. The state reorganized and controlled religions, and it instituted widespread censorship. Thousands of Vietnamese with ties to the Americans and the South Vietnamese government were sent to "reeducation" camps. There, they were subjected to hard labor and often tortured.

In 1977 a second wave of immigration began as hundreds of thousands more Vietnamese began to emigrate from the country. Some escaped by land, traveling through Cambodia or China. Many more tried to leave by sea. Packed in small, unsafe, wooden boats and carrying meager supplies, these Vietnamese became known as "boat people." As many as half a million boat people did not survive the attempt to escape. They perished at sea from drowning or as victims of piracy.

The plight of the boat people drew international attention. To help them, the United Nations High Commission for Refugees (UNHCR) set up refugee camps in neighboring countries, including Malaysia, Thailand, Hong Kong, Indonesia, and Singapore.

The Commission also helped negotiate the Orderly Departure Program (ODP) with the Vietnamese government. This program, instituted in 1979, enabled many Vietnamese to leave the country if they had relatives living in a host country who would sponsor them. As a result of the ODP, an estimated 100,000 Vietnamese refugees were eventually resettled in the United States.

POLITICAL REFUGEES

In the late 1980s, the U.S. government negotiated an agreement with the Vietnamese government to allow the release of detainees in reeducation camps and allow them to resettle in the United States. After Humanitarian Operation, or H.O., became effective in 1990, Vietnamese political prisoners were allowed to come to the United States. The criteria for release included length of detention and reason for detention. Family members of former prisoners were also allowed to leave.

As a result of the H.O. Program, Vietnamese immigration reached another high point in 1992, when more than 77,000 entered the United States. From 1981 to 2000, more than 530,00 Vietnamese were allowed to enter the United States.

DEALING WITH PREJUDICE

In the 1970s newly arriving Vietnamese immigrants were sometimes met with anger and resentment from Americans who had personally been affected by the long, drawn-out war in Vietnam—it had claimed nearly 60,000 American lives. Other U.S. citizens, fearful of losing jobs to the newcomers, disapproved of allowing the Vietnamese into the country. A Gallup poll taken in May 1975 showed that only 36 percent of Americans favored Vietnamese immigration to the United States. A full 54 percent were opposed.

Ethnic tensions between Vietnamese fishermen and their American counterparts along the Gulf Coast in Texas erupted in violence during the 1980s. For many Vietnamese in the area, it was a dangerous time as their homes were firebombed, boats

◀ CROSS-CURRENTS ▶

The United States is a land of immigrants, yet the arrival of newcomers has sometimes been viewed in a negative way. To see how Americans' opinions on overall immigration to the United States have changed over the years, turn to page 50.

were burned, and fishing nets were cut. It took many years, but eventually the two sides worked out their differences.

VIETNAMESE COMMUNITIES

Today, the states with the largest numbers of foreign-born Vietnamese are California and Texas. In fact, more than half of foreign-born Vietnamese live in these two states. Other states with large Vietnamese-American populations include Washington, Virginia, Massachusetts, Florida, Pennsylvania, and New York.

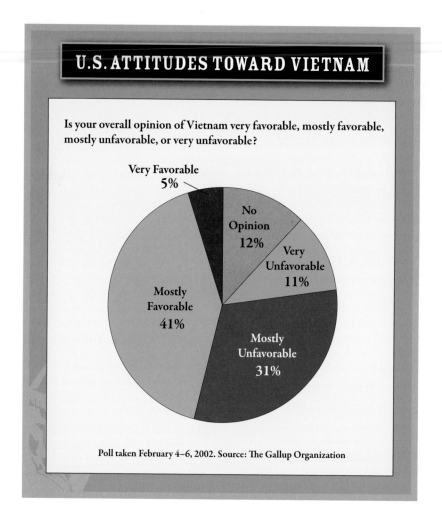

U.S. ATTITUDES TOWARD VIETNAM

Is your overall opinion of Vietnam very favorable, mostly favorable, mostly unfavorable, or very unfavorable?

Very Favorable 5%

No Opinion 12%

Very Unfavorable 11%

Mostly Favorable 41%

Mostly Unfavorable 31%

Poll taken February 4–6, 2002. Source: The Gallup Organization

Part of the city of Westminster, which is located in southern California, near Los Angeles, boasts a Vietnamese-American population of more than 200,000. Known as Little Saigon, after the former capital of South Vietnam, the district contains the largest Vietnamese population outside Vietnam itself.

On April 29, 2005, in Westminster, California, Vietnamese immigrants commemorate the 30th anniversary of the end of the Vietnam War.

CHAPTER TWO

Le Ly Hayslip: Humanitarian

By the time she was 20 years old Vietnam native Le Ly Hayslip had been subjected to more pain, suffering, and tragedy than most people face in a lifetime. Rather than become bitter, however, she channeled her energies in a positive direction. Since coming to the United States and becoming a citizen in 1978, she has devoted herself to helping others rebuild their lives the way she has rebuilt hers. Her efforts have helped people in both the United States and Vietnam heal the wounds caused by the war that devastated her native land.

A HORRIFIC CHILDHOOD

Le Ly Hayslip was born Phung Thi Le Ly on December 19, 1949. She was the seventh child in a Buddhist peasant family that lived in the farming village of Ky La, near Danang, in central Vietnam.

The desire to help others affected by the Vietnam War led Le Ly Hayslip to found a humanitarian organization in 1988 called East Meets West Foundation.

At the time of Le Ly's birth, her homeland was under French colonial rule. In an effort to achieve independence, rebels led by Ho Chi Minh were fighting a guerrilla war against the French. Le Ly's family, like most of the peasants, supported the rebels, who were known as the Viet Cong. The young girl acted as a lookout for them, and even helped dig their tunnels. Two of her brothers volunteered to fight with the Viet Cong. "We fought against the French, the Japanese and the Americans," says Hayslip. "We were fighting for our independence."

The French armies persecuted the villagers for helping the Viet Cong, while the Viet Cong came to believe that the villagers had betrayed their cause. Many villagers were killed. Over the course of time Le Ly herself was threatened, beaten, tortured, arrested, and sentenced to death by the rebels. Instead of being killed, however, 15-year-old Le Ly was raped by those in charge of her execution, and then set free.

During the Vietnam War, local villagers were often caught in the middle during conflicts between Viet Cong and American soldiers. In this March 1966 photograph war refugees are transported from their village by helicopter to safety.

Le Ly Hayslip: Humanitarian

SURVIVAL

Le Ly and her mother fled from Ky La and eventually settled in Saigon, the capital of South Vietnam. There, they worked in the household of a wealthy Vietnamese businessman. After Le Ly became pregnant by her employer, she and her mother were turned out onto the streets. They spent the next few years living in Danang and Saigon, together with Le Ly's infant son, James.

Life was hard and Le Ly did whatever she had to in order to survive. At various times she hustled souvenirs, black market items, and drugs. She eventually was able to find work as a nurse's assistant in a Saigon hospital.

COMING TO AMERICA

In 1969 Le Ly met and married an American contractor named Ed Munro. She was just 20 years old, and Munro was much older. The following year she came to America with her husband, and soon gave birth to his son, Thomas. However, the marriage did not last long. Three years later Munro died of emphysema. At age 24 Le Ly was a widow with two young sons.

In 1974 Le Ly married her second American husband, Dennis Hayslip. A year later, as the Vietnam War was coming to an end, he went to Vietnam to find Le Ly's mother and sister Lan, and Lan's two children by an American soldier. He managed to find and rescue his wife's family, bringing them back to the United States along with him.

Dennis, however, had many problems of his own. He was a heavy drinker and was given to fits of depression and rage. In 1982 Le Ly could take no more. She began divorce proceedings. Unable to cope with his demons, Dennis committed suicide.

Before he died Dennis had established a trust fund for Le Ly. Using the money, she invested in real estate and the stock market. Her investments did quite well and enabled her to provide for her family, which now included three sons.

MEMOIRS

During the 1980s Le Ly began writing a memoir about her life in Vietnam. *When Heaven and Earth Changed Places: A Vietnamese Woman's Journey from War to Peace* was published in 1989 to rave reviews.

The book told about the childhood and war experiences of Le Ly. In the epilogue she summarized her story, writing:

> Right now . . . there are millions of other poor people around the world . . . who live their lives the way I did in order to survive. Like me, they did not ask for the wars that swallowed them. They ask only for peace—the freedom to love and live a full life—and nothing more.

The second installment of Hayslip's memoirs, *Child of War, Woman of Peace*, came out in 1989. This volume chronicled her life in the United States in the years after her arrival in 1970.

Both memoirs by Hayslip became best-sellers that are studied at schools and universities across the United States today. They have been published in at least 17 different languages. Award-winning director Oliver Stone brought her story to the screen in the 1993 movie *Heaven and Earth.*

MAKING A DIFFERENCE

In 1986 Le Ly returned to her village of Ky La to see how her homeland had changed since the end of the war. She was shocked by the poverty and lack of medical facilities that she found. Determined

Hayslip poses with film director Oliver Stone, who in 1993 made the movie based on her memoir When Heaven and Earth Changed Places. *Also shown is Pham Thanh Cong, a Vietnamese consultant for a future movie project.*

to try to help the people of her native land, she established the nonprofit East Meets West Foundation in 1988. The organization provides funding for programs to improve health care and educational and vocational services for the Vietnamese people.

The East Meets West Foundation also works to normalize relations between Vietnam and the United States, an effort that has angered many anticommunist Vietnamese living in the United States. Because they do not favor normalizing relations with Vietnam, they have accused Hayslip of supporting a communist regime.

Le Ly also established the Global Village Foundation (GVF) in 1999. Based in the United States, this charitable organization works to provide educational and healthcare opportunities to children and rural villagers of Asia, including Vietnam. Programs funded by the organization have set up libraries, built schools, and provided emergency relief during natural disasters.

◄ **CROSS-CURRENTS** ►

Le Ly Hayslip has received many honors for her charity work, which has focused on trying to heal the wounds of the Vietnam War for the Vietnamese. Most forms of charity involve donating time, money, or goods to those in need. To learn more about charitable giving in America, turn to page 51.

CHAPTER THREE

Eugene H. Trinh: Astronaut and Scientist

In June 1992 Saigon-born Eugene Trinh became the first Vietnamese American in space. As a payload specialist, he flew on the 12th mission of the *Columbia* orbiter, the space shuttle carrying U.S. Microgravity Lab 1. Before and after that historic flight, Trinh worked as a research scientist at the Jet Propulsion Laboratory in Pasadena, California. He is currently director of the NASA Management Office at the Jet Propulsion Laboratory.

THE JOURNEY TO THE UNITED STATES

Eugene Huu-Chau Trinh was born in Saigon, Vietnam, on September 14, 1950. His father was a civil engineer who worked with the United Nations, the international organization that works to promote peace and cooperation among countries.

Payload specialist Eugene H. Trinh was the first Vietnamese American to travel into outer space.

When Eugene was just two years old, his father sent his family to live in France in order to avoid the violence in his homeland. Trinh's formative years were spent in Paris. He grew up speaking French and attending the city's public schools.

In 1968 Eugene graduated from Lycee Michelet, in Paris, with a baccalaureate in mathematics. Later that year he came to the United States, where he attended Columbia University, in New York City, on a full academic scholarship.

Trinh graduated in 1972 from Columbia with a bachelor of science degree in mechanical engineering–applied physics. He continued his graduate studies at Yale University, in New Haven, Connecticut, where he earned a master of science degree in applied physics in 1974, a master of philosophy in 1975, and a doctorate in applied physics two years later. Trinh remained at Yale working as a postdoctoral fellow for another year before taking a job at the California Institute of Technology (Caltech), in Pasadena.

MICROGRAVITY SCIENCE

The new job was at Caltech's Jet Propulsion Laboratory. Founded in 1944, this laboratory focused on the development and construction of rocket engines. It had been affiliated since 1958 with the National Aeronautics and Space Administration (NASA), the U.S. government agency responsible for the nation's space program.

Trinh specialized in the field of fluid mechanics, which is the study of fluids and the laws of physics that govern their motion. Some of his experiments were performed aboard the NASA KC-135 aircraft, which creates a reduced gravity environment known as microgravity. A brief period of weightlessness occurs aboard the KC-135 airplane when it ascends steeply, levels off, and then begins to dive.

SPACE SHUTTLE ASTRONAUT

In 1983 Trinh applied for and was accepted to serve as a payload specialist astronaut, working as a physicist on the space shuttle. Payload specialists are scientists with technical expertise selected for specific NASA missions. Trinh's expertise in microgravity research resulted in his selection as an alternate payload specialist for the 1985 mission of STS-51B *Challenger*. However when the flight took place he was not needed to serve as an alternate.

Trinh finally got his chance to go into outer space in 1992, when he served as a payload specialist on the space shuttle *Columbia*. When the STS-50/United States Microgravity Laboratory-1 Spacelab mission was launched on June 25,

The space shuttle, officially known as the Space Transportation System, or STS, consists of an orange external tank, two solid rocket boosters, and an orbiter. The orbiter carries astronauts and the mission equipment.

Trinh made history as the first Vietnamese American to travel into outer space. (The first Vietnamese in space was research cosmonaut Pham Tuan, who traveled to the Soviet Salyut 6 station on board Soyuz 37 in July 1980.)

During *Columbia*'s long flight Trinh and his fellow astronauts used the space laboratory to conduct more than 30 microgravity tests and experiments. The mission was the first extended duration orbiter flight. Previous missions typically lasted a week to 10 days. For this mission the *Columbia* orbiter remained in space for 13 days. It made 221 orbits of the Earth and traveled a distance of 5,758,000 miles.

The *Columbia* returned to Earth on July 9 at the Kennedy Space Center, in Florida. It had been originally scheduled to return to Edwards Air Force Base, in California, but the landing was switched to Kennedy due to Hurricane Darby, which threatened the California coast.

The mission provided new information on the effects of long-term reduced gravity on humans. Trinh's experiences convinced him that NASA must plan to sponsor both manned and

Space shuttle Columbia *crewmembers pose in the U.S. Microgravity Laboratory-1. From top to bottom and left to right are pilot Kenneth Bowersox, payload specialist Lawrence J. DeLucas, commander Richard N. Richards, payload commander Bonnie Dunbar, mission specialists Carl J. Meade and Ellen S. Baker, and payload specialist Eugene H. Trinh.*

unmanned flights in the future. Years after he left the astronaut group, he told a group of students at Yale:

> You can't put a human in space for more than six months without physiological deterioration. The bones and the immune system get weaker, so the amount of work that can be done on manned space missions is also limited. Robotic exploration is definitely going full blast, but there has to be a happy medium between manned and unmanned flights.

BACK ON EARTH

Trinh remained with the Jet Propulsion Laboratory until 1999. He then joined NASA as director of the Physical Sciences Research Division in the Biological and Physical Research Enterprise. The main focus of research centers on the effects of gravity on various physical, chemical, and biological systems.

In May 2004 Trinh received the Golden Torch Award, an award presented at the Vietnamese American National Gala (VANG) to distinguished Vietnamese Americans for their achievements and service to the community. At the award celebration, he spoke about how he felt when the *Columbia* flew over Southeast Asia and he spotted the Vietnamese coastline. The sight of his homeland, he said, had a strong impact: "Now I know that deep down, you never forget where you came from," he told the audience.

◄ **CROSS-CURRENTS** ►

About ten years after Trinh flew on *Columbia,* the orbiter was destroyed in a deadly accident. Despite the risks of the space program many Americans continue to support it, a Gallup poll has found. For more information, turn to page 52.

CHAPTER FOUR

Viet D. Dinh: Assistant U.S. Attorney General

On September 11, 2001, terrorists killed almost 3,000 people by flying airplanes into the World Trade Center towers in New York City and the Pentagon in Washington, D.C. In order to prevent such acts from happening in the future, legislation was passed giving the government greater surveillance powers. The chief architect of the legislation—known as the USA PATRIOT Act—was Assistant Attorney General Viet D. Dinh, who was born in Vietnam.

ESCAPE FROM VIETNAM

Viet D. Dinh was born in Vuang Tau, Vietnam, on February 22, 1968. He was the youngest of seven children born to Nga Thu Nguyen. His father, Phong Dinh, was a city councilman in his native land. When Vietnam fell to the communists, Viet's father was imprisoned in a reeducation camp. Viet was just seven years old at the time.

Three years later, in 1978, Phong Dinh escaped from the camp and became a fugitive. Meanwhile, Viet, his mother, and five of his siblings fled the country, together with 80 others, on a 15-foot-long boat. The refugees landed in Malaysia, where the government refused to accept them. Knowing they would be forced back to sea, Viet's mother took an axe and chopped a hole in the boat, causing it to sink. Dinh recalled,

> That image of my mother destroying our last link to Vietnam really stands in my mind to this day as to the incredible courage she possesses, but also the incredible lengths to which my parents, like so many other people, have gone to in order to find that promise of freedom and opportunity.

The Dinh family stayed for a few months in a refugee camp in Malaysia before making their way to the United States. They settled in Portland, Oregon, where they eked out a meager existence picking strawberries, trying to raise money to bring Viet's father to the United States.

When the Mount St. Helens volcano erupted in 1980, however, the family was forced to relocate. They moved to southern California, settling in Fullerton. Viet helped bring money in by working in a sewing shop and at a local eatery. In 1983 Phong Dinh was able to make it to the United States and rejoin the family.

Viet Dinh served as assistant attorney general of the United States from 2001 to 2003, in the administration of President George W. Bush.

Viet excelled at both Nicholas Junior High School and Fullerton High School. After he graduated from high school in 1986, he attended Harvard University on a scholarship, and then went on to Harvard Law School. Viet graduated magna cum laude from both.

IN THE PUBLIC EYE
After graduating from law school, Dinh clerked for U.S. Court of Appeals judge Laurence H. Silberman. The next year,

he did the same for U.S. Supreme Court judge Sandra Day O'Connor. In 1996 he joined the faculty of Georgetown University, where he taught constitutional law, corporate law, and the law and economics of development.

Dinh also became involved in politics, promoting a conservative agenda in the policy decisions being made in Washington, D.C. Like many Vietnamese refugees, he was attracted to the Republican party because of its strong anticommunist stance. He provided legal advice for Republican senators at congressional committee hearings and served as special counsel to Senator Pete V. Domenici during the impeachment trial of President Bill Clinton, in the late 1990s.

In May 2001 Dinh was named assistant attorney general in the Office of Legal Policy. In this position, he served as advisor to Attorney General John Ashcroft, in the administration of George W. Bush. Four months after Dinh became assistant attorney general, American were stunned by the catastrophic attacks by al-Qaeda terrorists.

THE SEPTEMBER 11 ATTACKS

Nearly 3,000 people were killed in the attacks by al-Qaeda, a radical Islamic organization led by Osama bin Laden. Following September 11, steps were taken to prevent similar acts from occurring in the future. Dinh explained in an interview with Bryant Gumbel:

> Right after 9-11, after the first National Security Council meeting, the President turned to the Attorney General and said very simply, "John [Ashcroft] you make sure this does not happen again." The Attorney General then turned to the men and women of the justice [department] and asked for a very carefully vetted set of proposals that would serve to prosecute the war against terrorism on the short term and to win that war in the long term.

In response to the September 11 attacks, which caused the destruction of the World Trade Center in New York City, Congress passed the Patriot Act. Viet Dinh helped develop the legislation.

Those proposals would eventually become known as the Uniting and Strengthening America by Providing Appropriate Tools Required to Intercept and Obstruct Terrorism Act of 2001 (USA PATRIOT) Act, also known simply as the Patriot Act.

THE USA PATRIOT ACT

In his position in the Department of Justice, Dinh undertook to reshape federal law to give enforcement agencies much greater power to track terror suspects. The Patriot Act reflected his effort to use all available resources to protect the United States from future attack.

Many civil libertarians, however, believed the Act granted powers that were too broad. They argued that it gave the government the power to spy on citizens

◀ **CROSS-CURRENTS** ▶

Immediately following the attacks of September 11, 2001, almost 60 percent of Americans worried that they or family members could be victims of terrorism, according to a Gallup poll. For more information, turn to page 53.

Viet D. Dinh: Assistant U.S. Attorney General

without having sufficient cause, thereby violating the Fourth Amendment to the Constitution, which guarantees privacy against unreasonable search.

Dinh, however, believes the law is misunderstood. He explains, "I think right now at this time and this place the greatest threat to American liberty comes from al-Qaeda and their sympathizers rather than from the men and women of

Viet Dinh testifies before the Senate Judiciary Committee on November 18, 2003, in Washington, D.C. The Senate was investigating aspects of the Patriot Act regarding its effect on Americans' civil rights.

President George Bush signs the act that reauthorized the Patriot Act in 2005. Many people believed its passage was essential to help the U.S. government combat terrorism.

law enforcement and national security who seek to defend America and her people against that threat."

Because of the Patriot Act's controversial nature, it has been amended and modified several times. Many of its provisions were to "sunset" beginning in December 2005. This means they would end unless further legislative action was taken to extend them. A reauthorization bill that included several changes was passed by Congress and signed into law by President Bush in March 2006.

Despite the controversy caused by the Patriot Act, Dinh makes no apologies for his work. He explains:

> In each and every thing that I do in my life . . . I ask myself how can I better serve the cause of freedom and the cause of good government. And while some may disagree with the decisions I make . . . I hope that people will recognize that there is . . . an honest effort of a person trying to serve his country at her time of greatest need according to his best ability, however limited that may be.

CHAPTER FIVE

Betty Nguyen: Television Journalist

Kim Nguyen wanted her daughter, Betty, to go into a field such as medicine, law, or engineering. But Betty had other ideas. She wanted to be a journalist. She followed her dream to the Cable News Network (CNN), where she became the network's first Vietnamese-American news anchor. Her success has given her the means to give back to her homeland, Vietnam, as a cofounder of the charitable organization Help the Hungry.

FROM SAIGON TO TEXAS

Betty Nguyen was born on October 10, 1974, in Saigon, Vietnam. Her father was an American serviceman and her mother was a Vietnamese college student. When Betty was less than a year old, her family fled from the country in a U.S. military cargo plane. They were first sent to refugee camps in the Philippines and Guam. They finally reached the United States at Camp Pendleton, near San Diego, California. From there, they eventually made their way to Texas, where they settled.

Betty Nguyen has served as a CNN anchor since joining the network in April 2004.

In April 1975 Vietnamese refugees headed for Camp Pendleton are processed at a passenger terminal. Nguyen's family was among those who settled in the United States after first spending time in the Camp Pendleton refugee camp.

Betty soon found her interests leading her down a path very different from the one her mother envisioned. While in high school Betty worked at a law office, but soon realized she did not see herself in a law career. In an interview, she explained:

> I always thought I would be a lawyer. Being Asian American, you drift to that—something that is a wonderful career and something of prestige. I tried working in an attorney's office in Arlington and I did not have a passion for it. I thought back and remembered that I really loved debate in high school, loved to write. And you know what, I went to the University of Texas and never looked back.

At the time there were few Asian news anchors on television, and none who were Vietnamese-American. Although Betty's mother was leery about the opportunities available for a person of Vietnamese descent, she was supportive of her daughter's decision to major in journalism.

THE ROAD TO THE TOP

Nguyen graduated from the University of Texas at Austin in 1995 with a degree in broadcast journalism. Because she worked in several internship positions while in college, she had connections who helped her get her first job after college.

Betty began her career as the morning anchor and reporter at KWTX in Waco, Texas. Her work earned her an Associated Press Award for spot news coverage. From there, Nguyen moved to KTVT in Dallas, where she worked for six years as a news anchor. During that time Betty continued to gain notice for her work. In 2003 she won the Legacy of Women Award and a regional Emmy for Outstanding Noon Newscast. That same year she also worked as a freelance correspondent for E! Entertainment Television during the California gubernatorial election.

One of the high points of her early years as an anchor, Nguyen would later say, occurred during her time in Dallas. She reported the story of a young boy who needed a corneal transplant in order to keep his sight. His family had no money, and the boy's chances for the operation looked slim. After Betty's report, however, a doctor in the area called and offered to do the surgery for free. The operation was a success and the boy retained his sight. She fondly remembers the incident as an example of how a journalist can affect a person's life.

A BIG BREAK

A turning point in Betty Nguyen's career came when she was offered a job as network anchor for CNN. The 24-hour television news channel is based in Atlanta, Georgia. Nguyen began May 1, 2004, on a CNN weekend program. With her warm, direct approach, she soon developed a devoted following. One Los Angeles fan explained: "I saw that there was this person who was very straightforward, with a lot of necessary information about things that I care about. She has chemistry."

The headquarters of Cable News Network is located at the CNN Center in downtown Atlanta, Georgia.

Betty currently coanchors *CNN Saturday Morning, CNN Sunday Morning*, and the weekend editions of *CNN Newsroom*. She also works as a correspondent covering issues and events from around the world.

In 2007 Nguyen was recognized by the Smithsonian Institute for her work as the first Vietnamese American to anchor a network television news broadcast. The institution featured her in an exhibit entitled "Exit Saigon, Enter Little Saigon." The exhibit, which opened in February 2007, commemorated the 30th anniversary of Vietnamese mass migration to the United States. It also told the stories of today's Vietnamese Americans.

BACK TO VIETNAM

In her career as a news anchor Nguyen has reported on some of the biggest news stories of recent years. They include the September 11 terrorist attacks, in 2001; the tsunami disaster in Southeast Asia, in December 2004, and Hurricane Katrina, which devastated New

◀ **CROSS-CURRENTS** ▶

The news media has undergone dramatic changes in how much trust audiences place in newspapers, TV, and radio. To learn more, turn to page 53.

The Web site for Help the Hungry.org. The global humanitarian aid organization was established in 2000 by Betty Nguyen and her family to help poverty-stricken rural areas in southern Vietnam.

Orleans, Louisiana, in August 2005. Her work has garnered her many awards and honors.

Serving as a news anchor and correspondent has also given Nguyen the opportunity to return to Vietnam, which she first did with her mother in 1998. Betty would later say that she was astonished at the conditions she found there. Villagers, who lived in grass huts with dirt floors, had barely enough food to survive. During the monsoon season, flooding caused hundreds of deaths.

Betty and her mother were determined to do something about the situation. In 2000 they founded Help the Hungry, a nonprofit organization that provides humanitarian aid to those living in poverty. As part of the program's mission, Betty returns to Vietnam every year, bringing food, clothing, medicine and other essential supplies along with her. "We've helped thousands during some of their most desperate times, she told one interviewer. "It's truly some of the most rewarding work I've ever done. I like to call it taking responsibility for my blessings."

CHAPTER SIX

Dat Phan: Comedian

Dat Phan came to the United States from Vietnam when he was still a toddler. Most of his early life in America was spent dealing with poverty and hardship. While chasing a dream of becoming a comedian, he worked at various odd jobs, including that of doorman at a comedy club. But he finally got his big break when he was chosen the winner on the first season of the television reality show *Last Comic Standing*.

HOMELESS

Dat Tien Phan was born in Saigon, Vietnam, on January 25, 1975. He was the youngest of 10 children born to Dung Thi Ho-Phan. When he was born, the communists were on the verge of taking over Saigon. The Phan family fled the city packed in the back of an ambulance.

Dat's family eventually made it to the United States, where they first landed in a refugee camp in Arkansas. From there, they went to Chicago, Illinois, where they lived for about five years. Dat's mother and father had separated by the time one of Dat's sisters got a job in a beauty salon in San Diego, California.

Dat's mother followed her daughter to San Diego, bringing Dat with her. They had difficulty finding his sister, however, and wound up living on the streets. "My mom and I lost touch with my family," explains Dat. "We ended up homeless. There were times we slept on bus stops in City Heights.

Dat Phan gives a performance in 2005 at the Ice House, a comedy club in Pasadena, California.

I was 5 or 6 years old. It was just me and my mom, we couldn't find the rest of my family."

Dat's sister eventually saved up enough money to buy a salon of her own in Santee, a suburb of San Diego. Dat and his mother finally made contact, and moved in with her.

THE ROAD TO COMEDY

Dat grew up in Santee, where he attended West Hills High School. After graduating, he took on odd jobs to bring in money for the family. At various times, he worked as a doorman, a bagger, a busboy, and a waiter.

Phan had been very quiet as a teenager. In an effort to overcome his shyness, he took a speech class at Grossmont

Community College in La Mesa. His experiences there ignited a desire to have a career in stand-up comedy. "I realized I was making people laugh during my speeches," he recalled, "and I liked that feeling."

Phan began going to a comedy club in La Jolla called the Comedy Store. One night he finally got up the nerve to sign up for an open mike session. Like most beginning comics, he struggled at first. He kept at it, though, refusing to give up. "I didn't do real well," says Dat. "I bombed. Something sick inside me told me to keep trying because I had nothing to lose. I gave it another shot, and I still bombed, but I got one laugh. And that laugh gave me encouragement to continue for the next seven years."

Phan was still making very little money in September 2001 when terrorists attacked the United States. The event had a soul-searching effect on him, he says: "The 9/11 attack woke me up and made me realize life is short. I decided it is now time to make a decision to either follow your dream or do what your parents say. I chose to follow my dreams."

LAST COMIC STANDING

In early 2002 Dat moved north to Los Angeles. He gave himself four years to get a job on a television show. Day-to-day living was still a struggle. For a while, he lived with a friend. He eventually had to leave, however, and wound up living out of his car for two months.

The following year Dat heard about a new NBC stand-up comedy reality show called *Last Comic Standing*. He submitted an application, went for an interview, and was selected. He eventually was chosen from a nationwide talent search as one of the 10 finalists.

◀ CROSS-CURRENTS ▶

Last Comic Standing is a television reality show that premiered in 2003. Reality shows have actually been around since the 1940s. To learn more, turn to page 54.

Phan and fellow comedian Anthony Steven Kalloniatis, better known as Ant, clown around at the awards show The Commies, *held in December 2003. Both appeared in season three of the reality show* Last Comic Standing.

The show followed the reality-TV format, in which 10 amateur comedians lived together in a house and were given various challenges. These included performing standup in a laundromat or entertaining a group of young children. Each week the studio or the television audience voted (by phone or Internet) on which contestants would meet in head-to-head competitions. The audience would then vote on who lost and should be voted off the show. The first show premiered on June 1, 2003.

Some of the contestants resented Dat because of his relative inexperience as a comedian. They complained that he relied too much on Vietnamese and Asian stereotypes in his act. The TV audience, however, felt differently. In August 2003 Phan was selected as the winner of the first season of *Last Comic Standing.*

A NEW LIFE

Winning *Last Comic Standing* brought Dat many more opportunities. He had appearances in August 2003 on *The Tonight Show with Jay Leno* and *The Late Late Show with Craig Kilborn.* In 2004 he had a half-hour special, *Comedy Central Presents: Dat Phan.* That was followed by a small role in the crime thriller *Cellular.* Phan also appeared on *The Wayne Brady Show* and *The West Wing,* as well as in the films *Love Is the Drug*

(2005) and *Spring Break '83* (2008). He provided the voice for characters in the animated television programs *Danny Phantom* and *Family Guy*.

Despite the success, Phan has said that his years of living in poverty have helped him keep his perspective on life. In an interview, he explained:

> I learned that money's not happiness. The more famous I am and the more money I make, the closer I stay to my family and friends that I've known since junior high school. True happiness to me is the connection with fellow human beings I've known for a long time.

CHAPTER SEVEN

Dat Nguyen: Pro Football Trailblazer

In 1975 the family of Dat Nguyen fled from the war in Vietnam, eventually settling in the Gulf Coast town of Rockport, Texas. Despite growing up in an environment of ethnic racism, Dat became a local football hero. He later went on to enjoy a successful seven-year career in the National Football League as one of the most popular players in Dallas Cowboys history.

ESCAPING FROM THE VIET CONG

Dat Nguyen's family consisted of his mother and father—Tammy and Ho Nguyen—and four siblings. In the early 1970s the family worked as shrimpers in the tiny fishing village of Ben Da on South Vietnam's Vung Tan Peninsula.

In April 1975, shortly before the Viet Cong overran their village, the Nguyens fled their home. They boarded a fishing boat in the middle of the night and escaped to Thailand. At the time, Tammy Nguyen was four months pregnant with Dat. The family eventually gained sponsorship and was flown to the United States. Dat was born in a relocation camp in Fort Chaffee, Arkansas, on September 25, 1975.

From Arkansas the Nguyens traveled a roundabout path. They lived briefly in Kalamazoo, Michigan, where a local Catholic church bought them a car. They drove it south, making stops at Fort Worth, Texas, and New Orleans, Louisiana, before finally settling in Rockport, on the Gulf Coast of Texas.

THE FACE OF PREJUDICE

The Nguyens decided on Rockport (which is the English translation of Ben Da, their home in Vietnam) mainly because of the fishing opportunities open to the family. And they had relatives there. Many other Vietnamese families also settled in Rockport so they could continue to make a living by shrimping.

Unfortunately, the growing numbers of Vietnamese immigrants in the region drew the wrath of the local fishermen. They feared the newcomers would take their jobs. In his biography, Dat recalled how in August 1979 tensions were running high when two Vietnamese fisherman shot and killed a local man in self-defense. Between 1979 and 1981 several Vietnamese were beaten. Others had their boats or houses burned. "There was a lot of tension," recalled Dat, "but we did the best thing: We just ignored it. I was always wondering why my parents would say to choose my friends carefully, to just stay with relatives. They couldn't trust anyone. People wanted to run us out of town."

The Nguyens refused to leave. Ho sold one of his shrimping boats and opened a small restaurant. When the eatery failed, he provided for his family by doing carpentry work and running a small marine supply shop.

TURNING TO SPORTS

When Dat was in seventh grade, his parents grew concerned that he was hanging out with friends who might lead him into trouble. So they gave Dat a choice: either change his ways or be sent away to boarding

Dat Nguyen, who was the first Vietnamese American in the National Football League, has worked since February 2007 as an assistant coach for the Dallas Cowboys.

school. Dat decided to straighten out. He directed his energies into sports, playing soccer, baseball, basketball, and football.

Although bigger than most Vietnamese, Dat was relatively small for a football player. While in high school he stood 5 feet 11 inches tall and weighed 231 pounds. What he lacked in size, however, he made up for with desire. He quickly became a star on the gridiron, playing both fullback and linebacker while leading his Rockport-Fulton High School team.

Negative attitudes toward the Vietnamese turned positive as Nguyen became the star football player at Rockport-Fulton High. Recalled Trish Wilson, who worked in the school district's central office, "He was a celebrity in high school. He was just one of those kids you don't see too often. If he was out there on the field, he was going to do something. He'd always get the extra yards, make the tackle, save the day." College coaches were soon knocking at his door.

THE MOST POPULAR AGGIE

Nguyen accepted a four-year scholarship to Texas A&M University, in College Station, Texas. In 1994 he was redshirted—that

Dat Nguyen, who had a close relationship with his mother, first played for Texas A&M during the 1995 season.

is, he was kept out of competition for a year in order to extend his period of eligibility to play in college. This gave him the opportunity to practice with the team while improving his skills.

The next year as a redshirt freshman he led the squad in tackles. As a sophomore Dat was named to the All-Big 12 Conference team. His junior year he won defensive Most Valuable Player honors while helping his team play in the January 1998 Cotton Bowl.

By the time Nguyen graduated with a degree in agricultural development, he was the Aggies' all-time leader in tackles. He capped his career by receiving All-American first team honors during his final football season, in 1998. That year he also won the Vince Lombardi Award as the Outstanding College Lineman of the Year, and the Chuck Bednarik Award as the College Defensive Player of the Year.

Linebacker Nguyen celebrates during a November 1998 game at Kyle Field, home of the Aggies, in College Station, Texas.

Dat Nguyen: Pro Football Trailblazer

ON TO THE PROS

Despite his success in college, Nguyen had no guarantee that he would play in the National Football League (NFL). Many pro scouts who doubted his chances thought he was not big enough to play in the NFL. However, the Dallas Cowboys selected him in the third round of the 1999 NFL draft.

Dat spent most of his rookie season on the special teams squad. The next year he won the starting middle linebacker job. Demonstrating great speed and range for the position, he endeared himself to Cowboys fans with his hard-nosed approach to the game. In 2001 he came into his own, starting all 16 games and recording 172 tackles. At the time, that was the second-highest single-season tackle total in Cowboys history.

In 2002 injuries limited Dat to eight games. He bounced back in 2003 with a solid year under the newly hired coach Bill Parcells. Nguyen again led Dallas in tackles that season, and he

In 1999 the Dallas Cowboys drafted Nguyen, who wore number 59. He played for the team until 2005, when a neck injury forced an early retirement from the game.

Dat Nguyen (right) joins Dallas Cowboys owner Jerry Jones (left) during an August 2006 ceremony honoring the NFL trailblazer at Texas Stadium in Irving, Texas.

was named to the first team All-Conference squad by *Pro Football Weekly*. The following year Nguyen repeated his success by leading the Cowboys in tackles for the third time.

EARLY RETIREMENT

Dat's NFL career was cut short by a neck injury that occurred early in the 2005 season. After playing against the Denver Broncos on Thanksgiving Day that year, he met with coach Parcells and told him that the neck injury was keeping him from being able to play up to his high standards. He officially retired in 2006.

However, in February 2007 Nguyen returned to the scene of his professional football triumphs when Cowboys' head coach Wade Phillips hired him as defensive quality control coach and assistant linebackers coach. Dat brings to the job the same intensity and will to succeed that helped him overcome the odds to become one of the top defenders during his time playing in the NFL.

◀ CROSS-CURRENTS ▶

Dat Nguyen has established a career in the most popular sport in the United States, according to the Gallup Organization. To learn what other sports are among Americans' top favorites, turn to page 55.

CHAPTER EIGHT

Maggie Q: Actress

The child of a Vietnamese mother and an Irish-Polish-American father, Maggie Quigley was born and raised in Hawaii. As a young girl she dreamed of becoming a veterinarian, but Maggie's life took a different path. She became a model and top action film star in Hong Kong, where she was known as Maggie Q. Soon afterward, she made the transition to Hollywood movies, appearing in blockbusters with such actors as Tom Cruise and Bruce Willis.

THE ROAD TO HONG KONG

Maggie Denise Quigley was born in Honolulu, Hawaii, on May 22, 1979. Her mother, who is Vietnamese, was a bartender who became a property investor. Her father met his wife during the war in Vietnam. His profession remains something of a mystery to Maggie. "He worked for the government," she told an interviewer. "I don't know what, specifically, he did. I know he was some kind of investigator."

Maggie was the youngest of three girls born to the couple. The family also consisted of two older children from Maggie's mother's first marriage. The girls grew up in the town of Mililani, on the island of Oahu. As a teenager Quigley was very athletic and starred on the Mililani High School track team.

After graduating from high school, 17-year-old Maggie decided to go to Asia to earn money. She planned to help pay for college by modeling. Her first stop was in Japan, but she had little success finding jobs there.

Quigley next tried Taiwan. There she met a woman who put her in touch with Meeyian Yong, who worked out of Hong Kong. By 1998 Maggie had settled in Hong Kong, and Yong was her manager. Quigley's height, at 5 feet 6 inches, limited her modeling opportunities—most models were much taller. However, Yong found work for Maggie doing commercials.

Actress Maggie Q is American-Vietnamese with Irish and Polish from her father's side.

Maggie Q: Actress

MAGGIE Q

Maggie's big break came when she was selected for a photo shoot with pop singer Nicholas Tse. This time her height helped her land the job—she had been chosen to appear with the Hong Kong celebrity because she was shorter than he was. The photo shoot with Tse brought Maggie to the attention of the Hong Kong media. It was at this time that Maggie Quigley became Maggie Q. She explains:

Maggie found new opportunities in Hong Kong (left) as a model. But it was after martial arts film star Jackie Chan (right) discovered her that she launched a successful acting career.

When I was living and working in Hong Kong, one of the biggest newspapers there when they first started writing about me . . . they could not pronounce my last name so they printed Q, Maggie Q, and so because they were the biggest [paper] everybody followed them. [It's Quigley] but, in Asia, everyone knows me as Q. I would show up to events, and everyone would say "Maggie Q," and I was like, "Oh, okay. Guess that is my name."

Within a short time Maggie Q was one of the top models in Hong Kong. She landed contracts with several major firms, including Coca-Cola, Shiseido cosmetics, and the luxury fashion companies Lancel and Louis Vuitton.

MODEL TURNED ACTRESS

The modeling assignments eventually brought Maggie to the attention of martial arts film star, Jackie Chan. In addition to working in Hong Kong and Hollywood as an actor, Chan is also an action choreographer, film director, and producer. When he approached Maggie about working in one of his films, he was surprised by her response. "I initially said no," she explained in an interview. "In Asia, when Jackie's company approaches you, you say yes. But I didn't know that I would be any good and I didn't want to disappoint anyone."

Maggie soon changed her mind. In an interview she later explained why she decided to leave modeling and pursue acting:

> I'm the kind of person who takes each day as it comes along. Some people have long-term plans, but I don't. It's a lot more challenging this way, but it also means I'm not stuck in one place. I want to give myself options—people in the business do that—I'm realistic, I can't be a cover girl forever. It's not a problem for me.

In the early 2000s Maggie became an action star. She was featured in several films made in Hong Kong, including the action thrillers *Gen Y Cops* and *Manhattan Midnight*. She had a cameo in the comedy *Rush Hour 2*, which starred Jackie Chan and Chris Tucker. Over the next four years, she appeared in eight more Hong Kong action thrillers. Her work in movies and magazines led the

◀ CROSS-CURRENTS ▶

After working and training for many years with Jackie Chan's team, Maggie Q became an expert in martial arts. For more information about this form of combat, turn to page 54.

Director J. J. Abrams poses with actors Tom Cruise and Maggie Q at a May 2006 screening of Mission: Impossible III.

men's magazine *Him* to vote her the most desirable woman in Hong Kong.

BACK TO AMERICA

With her movie career in Hong Kong at a high point, Maggie began to get offers from film studios in the United States, Britain, and Japan. One offer that came to her attention was for a role in *Mission: Impossible III*, starring Tom Cruise. Maggie auditioned for the part and won it, in part because of her athletic abilities and martial arts skills. As the only female member of the *Mission Impossible* team, she received a great deal of media attention after the 2006 hit was released.

Next came a part in the summer 2007 blockbuster *Die Hard 4: Live Free or Die Hard,* which starred Bruce Willis. Maggie played a villainous cyberterrorist who gets plenty of fight scenes.

Not wanting to be typecast in martial arts roles, Maggie has begun to branch out into other films. In 2007 she appeared in the action comedy *Balls of Fury*, which also starred Christopher Walken and George Lopez. In the film she plays the niece of a table tennis master.

In addition to appearing in Hollywood films, Maggie has continued to star in movies made in Asia. In 2007 she returned to China to film the historical saga *Three Kingdoms: Resurrection of the Dragon*. Released in April 2008 in China, the movie is based on a 14th-century Chinese classic called *Romance of the Three Kingdoms*.

Away from the camera, Maggie spends most of her time with her first love—her dogs. From her home in Los Angeles, she also works as an animal-rights activist. In 2007 she co-produced an animal-rights documentary called *Earthlings,* which is narrated by Joaquin Phoenix.

CROSS-CURRENTS

ATTITUDES TOWARD IMMIGRATION

The Gallup Organization surveys people around the world to determine public opinion regarding various political, social, and economic issues. One issue that Gallup has researched over the years is immigration to the United States. In general, Americans have a positive view of immigration, reports the Gallup Web site:

> Three in four [Americans] have consistently said it has been good for the United States in the past, and a majority says it is good for the nation today. However, Americans still seem interested in limiting the amount of immigration.

When asked in a July 2008 Gallup survey about the level of immigration into the United States, 39 percent of Americans favored decreasing the number of immigrants allowed into the country, a decrease from 45 percent a year earlier. However, only 18 percent believe it should be increased.

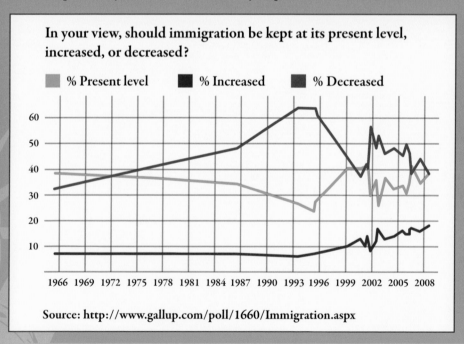

In your view, should immigration be kept at its present level, increased, or decreased?

■ % Present level ■ % Increased ■ % Decreased

Source: http://www.gallup.com/poll/1660/Immigration.aspx

CHARITABLE GIVING IN AMERICA

A 2003 Gallup reported that the majority of Americans (82 percent) had given money to charity sometime during the previous year. The following chart provides further details about how people in the United States contribute to charitable causes:

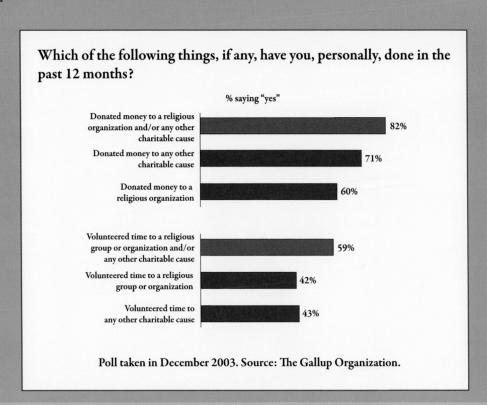

Which of the following things, if any, have you, personally, done in the past 12 months?

% saying "yes"

Donated money to a religious organization and/or any other charitable cause	82%
Donated money to any other charitable cause	71%
Donated money to a religious organization	60%
Volunteered time to a religious group or organization and/or any other charitable cause	59%
Volunteered time to a religious group or organization	42%
Volunteered time to any other charitable cause	43%

Poll taken in December 2003. Source: The Gallup Organization.

RISKS OF THE SPACE PROGRAM

The shuttle *Columbia* was the first spacecraft in NASA's Space Transportation System (STS). It first launched on April 12, 1981. Eugene Trinh flew on the orbiter during its 12th mission, in June and July 1992.

The *Columbia* made its 28th—and final—launch on January 16, 2003. The crew for that mission consisted of commander Rick Husband; pilot William McCool; mission specialists Michael P. Anderson, Laurel B. Clark, David M. Brown, and Kalpana Chawla; and payload specialist Ilan Ramon, of Israel. As the ship reentered the atmosphere on February 1, it disintegrated, killing all seven of its crewmembers.

Investigators determined that a piece of insulation that had broken off at launch made a hole in one of the craft's wings. During the orbiter's reentry, hot gases penetrated the wing, causing the ship's destruction.

Following the tragedy, some people called for an end to the space shuttle program. They believed the risks involved in the program outweighed the potential gains. In a 2003 Gallup poll, however, more than 81 percent of respondents said the United States should continue the manned space shuttle program. In the same survey, fewer than 9 percent of those polled said the amount of money spent on the space program should be decreased, while nearly 24 percent favored an increase in the amount of money spent.

Official crew photo from Mission STS-107. From left to right are David Brown, commander Rick Husband, Laurel Clark, Kalpana Chawla, Michael Anderson, pilot William McCool, and Ilan Ramon.

THE THREAT OF TERRORISM

Since the attacks on the World Trade Center and the Pentagon on September 11, 2001, the threat of terrorism has remained a major concern of most Americans. A 2004 Gallup poll asked respondents how they viewed international terrorism. Nearly 82 percent said they considered it a "critical threat," with 15.5 percent viewing it as an "important but not critical threat." Only 1.3 percent of those asked said that international terrorism was "not an important threat at all."

However, most Americans today do not believe they or their families are in personal danger. When asked whether they worried that they or someone in their family would become a victim of a terrorist attack, most Americans reported in a September 2008 Gallup poll that they did not fear being affected. Only 38 percent were "very" or "somewhat worried" that they or a family member would become a victim of terrorism. This percentage is less than the 47 percent who were worried in July 2007, and the high of 59 percent who were polled in October 2001.

PUBLIC CONFIDENCE IN THE NEWS MEDIA

Public confidence in the news media has fallen significantly over the past few years. A September 2008 Gallup poll asked the question, "In general, how much trust and confidence do you have in the mass media—such as newspapers, TV and radio—when it comes to reporting the news fully, accurately, and fairly?"

Only 9.2 percent of the respondents said they had a "great deal" of confidence and 34 percent a "fair amount." More than 55 percent of those questioned said they had either "not very much" confidence or "none at all." Just three years ago, the same question drew responses of 12.9 percent for a "great deal," 36.8 percent for a "fair amount," and 49.6 percent for either "not very much" or "none at all."

Even CNN, the self-proclaimed "most trusted name in news," has seen a decline. A Pew Research Center poll reported that the percentage of people who "believe all or most" of what CNN reports dropped 12 points, from 42 percent in 1998 to 28 percent in 2006. However, according to the study, compared to the other television news sources CNN remained the most trusted source for information.

TELEVISION REALITY SHOWS

Reality television has seen a tremendous increase in popularity since 2000. Shows such as *Survivor, American Idol, Dancing with the Stars, The Apprentice,* and *Big Brother* have all been successful—not just in the United States, but also abroad. Such shows generally place ordinary people, rather than actors, in supposedly unscripted situations.

Reality television actually dates back to 1948 when *Candid Camera* made its debut. Allen Funt's popular show featured the reactions of everyday people to pranks. In 1973 *An American Family* was a 12-part series that followed the lives of members of an average family going through a divorce. Police catching and arresting criminals was the theme of *COPS*, which debuted in 1989.

Although most of today's reality show contestants quickly disappear from the public eye, several have gone on to make a splash in the entertainment industry. *Survivor: The Australia Outback* contestant Elisabeth Hasselback became a host of the morning TV show *The View*. *American Idol* winners Kelly Clarkson, Ruben Studdard, Fantasia Barrino, Carrie Underwood, Taylor Hicks, Jordin Sparks, and David Cook have all gone on to musical careers with varying degrees of success.

THE MARTIAL ARTS

The martial arts are any system of practices and training for the purpose of combat. The word *martial* is derived from Mars, the name of the Roman god of war. The martial arts are also practiced for both physical and spiritual improvement.

Although different forms of martial arts have developed in every corner of the world, in the United States the term is generally associated with the systems that come from the Far East. These include judo, jujitsu, karate, kung fu, aikido, and tae kwon do.

The martial arts have gained popularity in the United States since the mid-1950s, when military personnel who were stationed in China, Japan, and Korea were exposed to the disciplines. They brought their knowledge of the skill back with them when they returned home. Experts like Chuck Norris and Bruce Lee promoted the combat form in movies and on television in the 1960s and 1970s. Today, Jackie Chan and Jet Li continue to impress audiences with their skills on the big screen.

Many Americans practice various forms of the martial arts for self-defense. As of 2003, there were more than 1.5 million practitioners in the United States.

POPULAR SPORTS IN THE UNITED STATES

In the United States, baseball is referred to as "the national pastime." If the polls are to be believed, however, it has been replaced by football as the country's favorite sport. In a 2006 Gallup poll that asked, "What is your favorite sport to watch?" football led the list. In fact, more than 42 percent of the respondents selected it as their favorite. Football was followed by basketball (11.7 percent), baseball (11.2 percent), and auto racing (3.9 percent).

A Harris Interactive online survey also taken in 2006 gave similar results. Pro football led the way, with 29 percent saying it was their favorite sport. Next in line were baseball (14 percent), college football (13 percent), auto racing (9 percent), and men's pro basketball (7 percent).

Both the Gallup poll and Harris Interactive survey were aimed at adults. *USA Today* conducted a similar survey among kids in 1996. In this case, basketball topped the list as the "Favorite Sport to Watch." Football finished second, followed by gymnastics at third. Baseball or softball came in at eighth place.

The *USA Today* survey also broke down the results by gender. Football and basketball ranked first and second, respectively, with the boys, with baseball/softball and wrestling tied for third. Girls, on the other hand, voted gymnastics their favorite sport, followed by basketball and skating.

The sport of football draws a huge crowd. The NFL reported that the league had an average of more than 67,000 fans at the 256 games that occurred in 2007.

NOTES

CHAPTER 1

p. 7: "Charges were made that removing . . ." Quoted in Allison Martin, "The Legacy of Operation Babylift," Adopt Vietnam. http://www.adoptvietnam.org/adoption/babylift.htm

CHAPTER 2

p. 13: "We fought against the French . . ." Quoted in "Vietnamese Author Visits UNF Students," Inside UNF (University of North Florida) Online, October 18, 2004. http://www.unf.edu/development/news/insideunf/02%20march/Award.html

p. 15: "Right now . . ." Le Ly Hayslip and Jay Wurts, *When Heaven and Earth Changed Places* (New York: Plume, 1990), 366.

CHAPTER 3

p. 21: "You can't put a human . . ." Quoted in "NASA Needs More Engineers, Says Alumnus Astronaut," *Yale Bulletin & Calendar*, April 18, 2003. http://www.yale.edu/opa/arc-ybc/v31.n26/story4.html

p. 21: "Now I know that deep . . ." Quoted in Anh Do, "The Big Show," Nguoi Viet Online, May 13, 2004. http://www.nguoi-viet.com/absolutenm/anmviewer.asp?a=4187&z=9

CHAPTER 4

p. 23: "That image of my mother . . ." Quoted in Yian Q. Mui, "From East to West, Then Up and to the Right," Hung Nguyen, August 29,

2001. http://www.hungnguyen.com/PRNews/news_082901.htm

p. 24: "Right after 9/11, after the . . ." "Sacrifices of Security: Patriot Act Debate," Flashpoints USA, July 15, 2003. http://www.pbs.org/flashpointsusa/20030715/infocus/topic_03/trans_pat_act.html

p. 26: "I think right now at . . ." Quoted in Kim Zetter, "The Patriot Act Is Your Friend," Wired, February 24, 2004. http://www.wired.com/politics/law/news/2004/02/62388?currentPage=all

p. 27: "In each and every thing . . ." Quoted in Kim Zetter, "The Patriot Act Is Your Friend."

CHAPTER 5

p. 29: "I always thought I would . . ." Ahn Do, "CNN's First Vietnamese Voice Attracts Asian Audience," Pacific News Service, November 30, 2004. http://news.pacificnews.org/news/view_article.html?article_id=922ada5cd5ff0af94be7cc53299fee70

p. 30: "I saw that there was . . ." Ahn Do, "CNN's First Vietnamese Voice Attracts Asian Audience."

p. 32: "We've helped thousands . . ." Jaymie Moran, "CNN's Betty Nguyen," Asiance, May 2008. http://asiancemagazine.com/may_2008/cnns_betty_nguyen

CHAPTER 6

p. 33: "My mom and I lost . . ." Quoted in Robert P. Laurence, "Dat's Funny, But It's Been a Long Road to Get There," *The San Diego Union-Tribune*, June 23, 2003. http://www.signonsandiego.com/

entertainment/remote/20030623-9999_1c23remote.html

p. 35: "I realized I was making . . ." Quoted in Robert P. Laurence, "Dat's Funny, But It's Been a Long Road to Get There."

p. 35: "I didn't do real well . . ." Quoted in Robert P. Laurence, "Dat's Funny, But It's Been a Long Road to Get There."

p. 35: "The 9/11 attack woke me up . . ." Quoted in Robert P. Laurence, "Dat's Funny, But It's Been a Long Road to Get There."

p. 37: "I learned that money's not . . ." Quoted in Larry Getlen, "Fame & Fortune: Dat Phan," *Bankrate.com*. http://www.bankrate.com/brm/news/investing/20031217a1.asp

CHAPTER 7

p. 39: "There was a lot of . . ." Quoted in Kevin Sherrington, "The Foreman of the Wrecking Crew," *The Sporting News* (August 31, 1998), 54.

p. 40: "He was a celebrity in . . ." Quoted in Adam Piore, "Breaking Down Barriers," *Newsweek* (January 8, 2001), Vol. 137 Issue 2, 54.

CHAPTER 8

p. 44: "He worked for the government . . ." Quoted in "Lithe Spirit," *The Sunday Telegraph*, June 17, 2007. http://www.telegraph.co.uk/fashion/main.jhtml?xml=/fashion/2007/06/17/stmaggie117.xml&page=1

p. 46: "When I was living and . . ." Quoted in Lynn Barker, "Maggie Q's Impossible Mission," *Teen Hollywood*, May 8, 2006. http://www.teenhollywood.com/d.asp?r=122843&c=1025

p. 47: "I initially said no. In . . ." Quoted in "Lithe Spirit," *The Sunday Telegraph*.

p. 47: "I'm the kind of person . . ." Quoted in Patsy Kam, "There's Something About Maggie," The Star Online, August 20, 2003. http://www.maggie-q.net/art1.html

CROSS-CURRENTS

p. 50 "Three in four . . ." "Immigration," Gallup.com, 2008. http://www.gallup.com/poll/1660/Immigration.aspx

GLOSSARY

Amerasian—a person of mixed American and Asian descent.

boat people—Vietnamese refugees who fled their country during the late 1970s and early 1980s by small boats.

communist—describing a form of government in which all property and businesses are publicly owned and controlled by the state.

emigrate—to move away from one's country to settle in another country or region.

Emmy—annual award given by the Academy of Television Arts and Sciences to recognize outstanding achievement in television.

gubernatorial—relating to the office of state governor.

guerrilla war—a conflict in which unconventional strategies and tactics are used by small groups of combatants.

immigrate—to move to and settle permanently in another country.

magna cum laude—with great distinction.

memoir—a written account of a person's life.

naturalization—process by which a person applies for and obtains U.S. citizenship.

open mike—a musical or comedy stage where anyone is invited to perform.

payload specialist—an individual trained to conduct specific experiments on a space mission.

physiological—relating to the way that living things function.

poll—a survey, often conducted over the phone, in person, or over the Internet, in which the public's attitudes about specific issues are documented.

propulsion—the force by which something is moved forward.

refugee—a person who flees from a country to escape war, persecution, or natural disaster.

surveillance—continual observation of a person or group suspected of doing something illegal.

Viet Cong—Ho Chi Minh's guerrilla forces in former South Vietnam.

FURTHER READING

Englar, Mary. *Le Ly Hayslip*. Chicago, Ill.: Raintree Publishers, 2005.

Ferry, Joseph. *Vietnamese Immigration*. Philadelphia, Pa.: Mason Crest Publishers, 2004.

Nguyen, Dat, and Rusty Burson. *Dat: Tackling Life and the NFL*. College Station, Tx.: Texas A&M University Press, 2005.

Pham, Quanq X. *A Sense of Duty: My Father, My American Journey*. New York: Ballantine Books, 2005.

Sinnott, Susan. *Extraordinary Asian Americans and Pacific Islanders*. New York: Children's Press, 2003.

Sonneborn, Liz. *Vietnamese Americans*. New York: Chelsea House, 2007.

INTERNET RESOURCES

www.cnn.com
The official Web site of the Cable News Network includes articles and videos of the news of the day in the fields of politics, crime, entertainment, health, technology, travel, business, and sports.

www.dallascowboys.com
The Dallas Cowboys professional football team features a variety of information, including team news, videos, rosters, biographies, statistics, history, schedules, and ticket and stadium information.

www.datphan.com
Comedian Dat Phan provides biographical and booking information, as well as information on stops along the Dat Phan tour.

www.gallup.com
The Web site of the Gallup Organization includes in-depth articles on issues and the results of polls taken by the international polling organization.

www.globalvillagefoundation.org
The official Web site of the Global Village Foundation gives information about the nonprofit charitable organization founded by Le Ly Hayslip.

www.nasa.gov
The official Web site of the National Aeronautics and Space Administration features articles and videos of past space missions and previews of those to come.

Tony Bui (1973–): Vietnamese-American film director. His 1999 film *Three Seasons* is the only film to win both the Audience Award and the Grand Jury Prize at the Sundance Film Festival. Bui also produced *Green Dragon*, starring Patrick Swayze and Forest Whitaker.

Anh "Joseph" Cao (1967–): The first Vietnamese-American member of Congress. Born in Saigon, the New Orleans lawyer was elected in 2008 to the House of Representatives, from Louisiana's second congressional district.

Kieu Chinh (1939–): Legendary actress whose career has spanned almost 50 years. Chinh is best known for her role in *The Joy Luck Club*, but she has also appeared in *A Yank in Vietnam* and *Operation C.I.A.* She cofounded the Vietnam Children's Fund, and has been active in philanthropic work.

Catherine Mai Lan Fox (1977–): Olympic swimmer who won gold medals in 400-meter freestyle relay and the 400-meter medley at the 1996 Summer Olympics in Atlanta, Georgia. Fox

Director Ham Tran (right) and actress Kieu Chinh attend the March 2007 premiere of his film Journey from the Fall.

is a 9-time National Collegiate Athletic Association champion and a 21-time All-American in swimming. In 2006 she was named to the Kansas Sports Hall of Fame.

Danny Graves (1973–): First Vietnamese-born player in the history of Major League Baseball. As a pitcher, Graves compiled 182 saves in 11 seasons with the Cleveland Indians, Cincinnati Reds, and New York Mets. He was selected for the 2000 and 2004 All-Star games.

Tony Quang Lam (1937–): First Vietnamese American to be elected to public office in the United States. Lam served three terms on the Westminster, California, City Council. He is also the owner of a restaurant in Garden Grove, California.

Duy-Loan Le (1962-): Engineer with Texas Instruments. Le is the first woman—and first Asian—to be elected TI Senior Fellow. She is active with many charitable organizations, and has been involved in building schools in rural areas of Vietnam.

Hau Thai-Tang (1966–): Chief program engineer for the Ford Motor Company on the 2005 Ford Mustang program. Thai-Tang oversaw the development of the Shelby GT500 while serving as director of Ford's performance vehicles division.

Ham Tran (1974-): Film writer, editor, and director. Of Chinese and Vietnamese ancestry, Tran has created award-winning works that explore the experiences of the Vietnamese during wartime and afterward.

Tran Dinh Truong (1932–): Principal owner of the largest shipping company in South Viet-

Born in 1973 in Saigon, pitcher Danny Graves is the son of a Vietnamese mother and American father.

nam, Truong made ships available to help evacuate refugees during the fall of Saigon in 1975. After immigrating to the United States, he owned and operated several hotels in New York City.

Huynh Cong Ut (1951–): Pulitzer Prize-winning photographer for the Associated Press. He won the award in 1973 for his photo "The Terror of War," which depicted children fleeing from a napalm bombing in Vietnam.

INDEX

Numbers in **bold italics** refer to captions.

PICTURE CREDITS

ABOUT THE AUTHOR

John F. Grabowski is a teacher and freelance writer from Staten Island, New York. His published work includes 50 books; a nationally syndicated sports column; and articles for newspapers, magazines, and programs of professional sports teams. He has also provided consultation on several math textbooks and sold comedy material to Jay Leno, Joan Rivers, Yakov Smirnoff, and numerous other comics.